Hurricane Catherine: A Book of Poetry

By Ryan Fredric Steinbeck

Copyright 2007 by Ryan Fredric Steinbeck. No part of this book may be reproduced, stored in a retrieval system or transmitted in any form or by any means without prior written permission of the publisher, except by a reviewer who may quote brief passages in a review to be printed in a newspaper, magazine, or journal.

ISBN: 978-0-6151-4757-4
Published by Ryan Fredric Steinbeck
www.ryanfredricsteinbeck.com

I'd like to thank Cindy, who is a constant inspiration for me each and every day.
Also thanks to Ricky and Sheena
This book is in loving memory of Mary and Irene Dohse, and Ryan Berger
I'd like to thank my family, Roger, Brenda, Shelly, Mike, Tom, Sandy, and all of my extended relatives, especially Ken(ny), without whom many of these poems would have never been written. Thanks to Matt, Rob and Mike.
Special thanks to the Collins' family

This book was written before, during, and after surviving two tropical storms and a hurricane in Florida. It was also written during a hurricane inside, which has lessened significantly. I've come to realize how important it all is to who I am becoming and where I ended up today. For that, I don't regret a single event.

These poems follow a sequence in time, almost like chapters in a book. If anyone reading has questions about meaning or anything else, contact me at my website.

www.ryanfredricsteinbeck.com   ryan@ryanfredricsteinbeck.com

Acknowledgements: People, events, poetry, novels and music and movies are constantly inspiring in my life. Thanks to everyone who has contributed, and expressed themselves through forms of media, and who continue to do so today. These include family, friends, strangers, and writers such as Robert Frost, W. B. Yeats, T.S. Eliot, Sting, U2, Jimi Hendrix, Prince, and countless others. There would be no me without them.

Table of Contents:

Hurricane Catherine
What it is
Beginning and End
World of Your Consequences
Story of You
I Had it All
Fade
An Honor
Lost Nation Road
Unfair
Gratuitous
A Thought About Saving the Universe
Move to Third
A View of Main Street
Gulf Breeze
Alexa
Late May
Far Gone
Stranded
The Corner
Destined Privileged Collision
Hole in the Water
Reunion
Confusion's August
The More I Despise
Dividing Mind
Dead Man's Creek
We Are Not In Love
Worlds Apart
Throwing Dice
Out of Season
My Problem Too
Hypnotized
Let You In
Something You Should Have Said
Light My Way
One More Day
Scapegoat and the Instigator
6 Days
You Just Don't Feel That Way Anymore
A Marching Army
Waiting
Leaving Florida

Right Time of Day, Right Time of Year
Begin
Nothing Underneath
Lack of Everything
Lost in the World
I Know Him, She Knows You
Nothing New
Season of Armistice
Happen
Final Chapter
In Hell
World of Excuses
Image of You
My Heart Left Town
The Way I Always Do
New Day
Within Reach
Faith in the Truth
Celebration and Tragedy
Photographs
One Road
Not a Dry Eye in the House
Smokescreen
Dual Identity
The Difference
The End of an Era
Series of Hypotheticals

Cover design by Michael R. Steinbeck.
Photos by Rachelle Poteracki and Cynthia Steinbeck. Special thanks to Rachelle Poteracki for the photos in Upper Level Disturbance, of which I never acknowledged.

HURRICANE CATHERINE

In it's early development
Lifting her from tropical depression
Gaining strength over my warm waters
Sudden landfall without warning
First Category 5 on record
Four years in duration
Shifting all directions
No survivors

Never before this interval
On to the 26th day
Experts forecasted this turn
Would finally put her to rest

Commitment constantly wavered
In early formation
The winds of change fell silent
I put down my last line of defense
I didn't notice her rebuilding
Until my power was knocked out

Pieces of my life scattered
Structures destroyed on shore
I work at renovation
But I need national assistance

One day I may understand
One day I might absolve
Today I only observe from shore
While it constantly changes course

Annihilating everything I worked for
On into the future
Causing more distant damage
Her storm may finally dissipate
But the devastation will remain
And I will never forget

WHAT IT IS

You try to shield my eyes from hurricanes
But I refuse to tip toe through time
You can't always hide my face from pain
It will only prevent the unavoidable

Don't hold it against her
Don't try and rationalize
No room for justification
We both know there is none to give

Sometimes it is what it is
I can only shift from day to day
The further I get the smaller your town appears
The sooner I arrive the more likely I'll stay

BEGINNING AND END

So this is the end, and the beginning
I'm one for the dramatic so excuse me
No way through without consequences
Unable to fake the existence

There is nothing more certain
At least that's the rational
A simple twist of fate
Has me in supposition
Somehow what was meant to be
Disentangled inexplicably
This fate must smooth itself out
Prepare for more catastrophes
Take shelter from more rain
Move from your cities and homes
Beware of the biggest hurricanes

Sadness, disillusionment
Anger and revulsion
Heartbreak and indiscretion
Hatred and distrust

Time will uncover incongruity
Truth will guide us to luminosity
If there is a cruel irony of fate
Then our story doesn't end correctly

I'm a beggar on your street
And I'm kneeling at your feet
With gold to offer you
But you only wish for silver

So this is the beginning
And this is the end
That it could have ever been different
I can only pretend

WORLD OF YOUR CONSEQUENCES

I am suspended
Though not above sorrow
It materializes in my region again

Sluggish are the days
A million hours until tomorrow
We are precisely where we've been

I live in the world of your consequences
I suffer the anguish you should feel
I regret the things you should not have done

I would believe your false pretenses
While beneath your pillars I kneel
I would endure a life of frigid nights
To wake up in your sun

STORY OF YOU

The moon and her lover hours away
I'm strewn across a petrified landscape
Hasty decisions and failed ideas
The lichen of my past builds on today's rocks

I keep falling awake at the wheel
As the story of you replays in my mind
So beautifully evil and cheap
Your mountain of excuses is too steep

In time there will be healing
I remain the only casualty in this disaster
I couldn't imagine another ending
That's more anticlimactic or faster

In high pursuit of lies
At least I was chasing something
My silence carries more weight that words
I save my sanity by saying nothing

A friend asked me if I'd lost my happiness
I said it was trying to get away
I put it in to storage and hid the key
So I can preserve it for a better day

It's a long way that we've come
After watching you from a distance
I noticed ignorance has a yellow hue
Yellow doesn't compliment you

Rumors fill the generational fairy tales
The ending turns dramatic
I've lived what has always been true
I know the real story of you

I HAD IT ALL

Amusing misfortune
Residue of surplus existence
Nine times out of ten the victor
As if I've slandered my own name

I ask and you answer
Nonchalant indifference
Subtle mode of conquest
Still hard to digest

One time there was more
To the summer and fall
To the oceans and seas
One time I had it all

Shattered truth in penitence
Throwing me off course
Your final hand I attempt to force
But it's hard to alter misdirection's source

Victimized standing here
By the naivety I possess
One more door that has become a wall
One time I had it all

FADE

Yesterday words exchanged
The mountains plummeted
I watched sandcastles crumble
Beneath your undulation

Warnings from the edifice
Not to change my pattern
On target to crash
Long before take off

Something meant to shine
Also meant to fade
To look one way in the sun
Yet differently in shade

All the cards are played
This insurmountable debt is paid
I would have chosen a different course
If the choice were mine to have made

A victim standing in judgment
Pleading guilty to reduce sentence
Banned to separate worlds
We carry the flags we've unfurled

Yesterday when words were exchanged
I knew you walked away
I knew this was how it will stay
I just didn't know I'd feel the same way

AN HONOR

If a fate can revolutionize
By differences of red and blue
Mine has been decided
Adjusting as I always do
Shorter distance than the last
Easier conversations
Irrefutable insecurities
I hesitate to hesitate

When the fires spread
When there is nothing left
When there is no turning back
I begin to move
Disciples planted in my path
Obstacles for my betterment
I'm supposed to live in rejection
Until rejection is absent

On a word it can change
From an unsuspecting purveyor
An intimidating history
With no reason for reverence
As the dialogue concludes
And the analyzing is through
For the first time in my life I hear
"It's an honor to meet you."

LOST NATION ROAD

Blue the Color
Split between two minds
Designation of a new institution
Ignoring the signs

It ends where it begins
A new wave of excuses
Reasons to put on armor
That never runs out of uses

The highlands of ancient times
Have fallen to lower levels of thinking
From beginning to end
Lost Nation Road

Such an authority
To commit legal transgression
Assurances of supremacy
As worldly intolerance and fear align

Within it a cultured pandemonium
Professionally designed
Emitting a frequency of triumph
Leisurely pronouncements secretly timed

Standing at the bottom of the hill
Making our way to the top
Slowly able to see a further landscape
Still we remain on Lost Nation Road

UNFAIR

Never to have opened your eyes
You didn't get an opportunity
The chance is gone
To know what it's like to fly

A cruel situation
Not the luck of the draw
The world was immeasurably unfair
A fate undeserving

What was the message?
I didn't read between the lines
I wouldn't understand if I did
No exposition is cogent

Maybe now you can fly
Take some fairness with you
Maybe there's a place for you in that line
Maybe good comes from this
Maybe when you finally open your eyes
Heaven is the place you will see for the first time

GRATUITOUS

An observation from this back street
I've sauntered here for years
Out of date, a blast from the past
As its milieu becomes larger than it
Attempting to hold onto proverbial
Only a sentiment internal
Reserved for a committee to decide
When to stop the bleeding
Embrace it or let go
How can I be home and still miss home?
Changes have proven inevitable
This is rapidly becoming gratuitous
Losing itself in itself
As I lose myself in it
Like a train with no scheduled stops
I can only look out and hope it slows down

A THOUGHT ABOUT SAVING THE UNIVERSE

As the Gods of war rephrase history
They find only one ambiguity
After everything we know is gone
How did we endure so long?

Attempting to construct the present from past
Based on ideas that will never last
Propagation of trepidation and intolerance
Born from voracity and ignorance

I don't hate myself or anyone else
I don't hate what we forget
I can't control the universe
But I would like to save it

MOVE TO THIRD

A new streetlamp on a new street
As you move further from where I am
Something more to covet
As you settle in
I am the reverse crescendo
Another proprietary gust
My representative secedes from the union
With no where else to go
I will concede the medal
I comply with the rules and regulations
I know it is supposed to be this way
Despite my obvious hesitations
I pass through our hall of fame
I see the tribute to our successes
Revered for the times we escaped trouble by inches
Our teamwork never ceased to impress
Looking up I see our ancient pedestal
Throughout our wing they've quoted every word
I pass through the way of old one last time
Then I step off second and move to third

A VIEW OF MAIN STREET

Gone astray on a thousand times road
The aerial view not deviant
Snow covered streets in summer
A few turns away but I cannot get there

Stopping at a local mercantile
Unobserved as if she can sense me
The enlightened outlook slowly putrefies
Minutes like a thousand days

A raised voice scarcely detected
Grudgingly, she makes her way back
Attempting to portray a native wisdom
My mind advances in a differing direction

With a vaguely stated solution, I step to the street
The cool breeze clears my head
I see a sign through snow cover
I feel like I'm a few streets over

There remains in me a crippling
I see the way but I freeze
Life is moving by me in the distance
I just can't get back there

GULF BREEZE

If in another time
When the tide is not as high
Illuminating schedules
Will not replace contact
An adventurous mind
A constant traveler
Grass always greener
In the land unknown

If I had been a sailor
If I had been a fisherman
If I had lived where the sun always warms the sky
Would the gulf breeze still call my name?

A hand in misdirection
A constant step ahead
Avoid the groundwork
Where real feelings lie
Several misconceptions
Compensation instead
True feelings always lurking
Opportunities keep passing by

If I had come from the south
From where I want to be now
If I had grown up with a blue back yard
Would the gulf breeze still call my name?
If I never sparred with cold
If winter was a foreign word
If I had never witnessed the flying south of birds
Would the gulf breeze still call my name?

If I had lived in the south
With a rocking chair facing the ocean
Would I be looking north?
Or would the Gulf Breeze still call my name?

ALEXA

Through cannon wars and trap doors
The only way to Alexa's house is up
Through rights of passage they get the message
The only way to go is up
The fallen down, the lost and found
With the right to live and the right to die
The right to keep and the right to solve
With open eyes and endless resolve

Alexa you will never know
All of the times I've seen you face to face
You don't know how much of you I see in me
I wish I could find some way
To believe in you completely
But I'm still looking for some mystery
An elusive ending I still have to chase
Despite the answers I find
My heart remains constant
Telling me the only way to go is up

LATE MAY

With a foreign tongue resembling late May
You breeze in with commentary
A waft and your gone before it sinks in
I am taken aback

Always a fallacy
The deciphering of words
Their trail left on screen
Leading to personal inference

I decide to take the offensive
Though it could mean the opposing
Extant is margin of error
As a weapon in safe keeping

Removal for emergencies
Rendering the lashing out unpardonable
Unable to be tacit
From this date it will stand between us

A pretense with compliments is ineffective
What remains is a visible barrier
Wedged between like a splint
We should call it off right now

FAR GONE

It feels like we are at war
Though you say we are at peace
Every benign statement
Turns into acts of aggression
A constant battle for territory
Hiding behind guilt and shame
Firing words as missiles
Hitting bulls eyes on every target
Still nothing gets resolved
Animosity only driven deeper
Into the cavernous depths from which it came
We have trouble finding its origination
Spreading like a cancer
Affecting other facets
Until it takes over
Peace talks like a comic story
That no one has heard before
Akin to a new concept
That will take years to develop
I'm afraid we don't have that much time
The breaking point has reached its breaking point
We are here trying to decipher
The codes to unlock determination
Like a siren in my head
There are always distractions
We are too far-gone now
I'm afraid we won't reach this peace
Until we go through war

STRANDED

I almost touched the clouds today
I could not find number nine
I did see elephants on their hind legs
Along with charging horses
I almost fell from the world today
I lost all concentration
I started second-guessing
Your face broke my descent

Stranded here without words
Stranded with time advancing
A deafening quiet outside
A crippling fear inside

Unsure why I stand here
Blinding confidence or lack of judgment
I've gotten ahead of myself
As I've left myself behind
A tourniquet around my patience
Tightening like a noose
One slip and I'm down for the count
As the cowards of the night break loose

Stranded one more time
Stranded when I thought I was found
Stranded and humbled by this difficulty
Stranded with everyone around

THE CORNER

I didn't allow for your permeation
Now I wish I had
As the sun set on my years with you
My fear of your freedom grew
I remember spending days thinking of futures
Unrealistic but within reach
You always knew more about the willingness to give
I gave into your determination to teach
But I always hid behind myself
A wall too high to climb
An opening you avoided at my beseech

I remember you as you stayed behind
Shedding layers of fear
Our importance in this ongoing saga
Has never become clear
Today I'm still standing in the center
I look around from time to time
You've walked away from this equation
Out of the corner in my mind

An effort of contact
Thwarted by jealous forces
Innocent intentions diluted by defection
The embankment of mishandled protection
Years imminent in this charade
Like a ghost you reappear in the corner
Just long enough to renew interest
Gone as sure as the blinking eye

Left with a bewildering curiosity
A sampling of truth and expectation
Your image flashes in the center
Maybe nowhere is your designation
I know it comes down to waiting
An attempt to trace the apparition's origin
For now I can only close my eyes to see
The corner of my mind that is dark and empty

DESTINED PRIVILEDGED COLLISION

Isolated sun banks on the horizon
Autumn grass falls asleep
Smells of freedom dominate
As I look over the hills

One way or the other
You are in the picture
A soul combination
In form of surprise

Hold onto that thought
Out with the eternity
What I found here
Matters more than I comprehend
We escaped with sanity
Living with uncertainty
There lies a future
That is ours for the taking

We moved together
The bridge holds us both
A destined privileged collision
In time of disorientation

A hint of foreshadowing
Invasion of territory
Unsuspecting
That time would come again

You are more to me
Than I could ever say
You are in my heart
Like no other
A small time found here
You impacted my soul
With distance far and wide
You always feel close

Return to sanity
Return to home
I'm the nomad in the world
As I travel alone
I see the stars
I know you have the same vision

I think of that summer
When the world came into view
What a privilege it has been
To know of you

HOLE IN THE WATER

Three times it has happened
In just one week
Reliving visions of the past
Startling accuracy

In the thick of timelessness
But lacking consistency
Are feelings floating to the surface
Along with voices of assurance

The crowd is chattering
Their visions are exhibition
I'm not sure what I should believe
I'm not convinced of the meaning

Always there is wonder
Two souls brought together
Negotiating a common interest
Despite the volatile weather

We jump into the water
With the storm threatening
Lightening on the horizon
Winds rapidly shifting

I know there is a reason
If one night should alter everything
If the storm should cross the nation
And those back home get information

Reality strikes like lightening
Truth as loud as thunder
To think it was ever possible
Is like a hole in the water

REUNION

Thousands of miles away
He sits on the edge of the ocean
England's been a good friend
She's taught him things he could never learn himself

Thousands of miles away
On the other side of the ocean
There are things she wants to tell him
Things she cannot write in a letter

Cold and lonely night
One more week remaining
She has been good company
As he looks at the itinerary of his flight

They speak of a different life
One were they might be lovers
But she knows of his wife
And his commitment to no other

But the ocean parts the land
Like the days between
And the distance we've constructed
Where has the time been?

Something in the voice
The resonance doesn't sound the same
Unconvincing the appeal
Uncertainties of the future begin
Vision and reality
Battle in their contrast
The only result is disappointment
He's seen things he could never read in a book

Putting ideas in motion
Sometimes a difficult science
She taught him how easy it could be
If he'd just stop waiting to be guided

Thousands of miles away
These are only thoughts in his head
Subtlety's been a good friend
Anxious for his return

Thousands of miles away
The distance has become her friend
For her a new day will begin
Their reunion a means to an end

CONFUSION'S AUGUST

I saw the city from the south for the first time
It was the other side of the moon
In early confusion's August
You were the other side of the moon

I saw the sky from underwater
I realized I was drowning
While swimming in August
In record cold

I saw the other side of you
It made me lose my faith
When August set in
It is usually a given
What you are going to get

Enter the cold of December
The chill of the oblivious
The carelessness of the ungrateful
The unheeding of the thoughtless
Everything built on prevarication

Gracing the year with such promise
Dissenting into objection
Faltering and unfounded
Treacherous without warning
Assassination of valued time

Here in the August of confusion
Confusion possesses no August
It is one violent circle
Replicating visits in my head

Reliving the visions
That my mind created
In the beginning of the end
When everything turned to gray

Outlast the inconsistency
Survive the naivety
Make it through the August of confusion
You're still in confusion's August

THE MORE I DESPISE

The sun is covered by smog
Acid rain burns the skin
Pavement covers land that once lived
Politics govern friendship

Ammunition replaces explanation
In the "no generation" generation
Decay and debris replace flourish
Abandonment of this warm home
Where all my memories still exist

No redemption or integrity
All solutions to all mysteries now gone
Each day a new disappointment
All hinging on the way you turn

A choice to live safely forever
Or to use the escape route
The fires you started burned too close
I can no longer extinguish

No more cure for anything
No more happiness after crying
The end of all the successes
All that's left is failure

Only you believe you
Within the realm of all your mendacity
The less you say the more I know
The more you give away the more I despise

DIVIDING MIND

There is not a love affair
That escapes my mind
There are no more shadows
That can see light

Waking up one day
No thinking or planning
Forward is the goal
Onward and upward

On a life long mission
Not to be a disappointment
Up until now
That is all I've seen

To this day I've wandered
Non-committal where I lay my head
Assured there will be changes before me
If nothing else

There are no answers
That seeking shall ever find
There is no movement
That can revolutionize the dividing mind

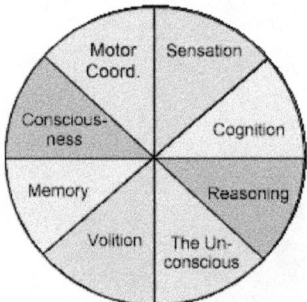

CATCHES UP

The way you turned the world
The way you were found out
The way you spelled it out
The way you fought the word
It catches up with you
The time you could have changed
The words you could have spoken
The effort you made
To have promises broken
The distance in your heart
The writing on the wall
The concealment of your pain
The mysteries you lost
The silence that you gain
The wisdom in your step
The heightened fear of love
The ghost of your words
The emptiness you never shared
The more you believe
The more it becomes
The way you do not care
The more you do not do
The time of mine you wasted
It catches up with you

DEAD MAN'S CREEK

We used to walk by Dead Man's Creek
With our truth hand in hand
It went by a different name
We went by a different name
I never thought this place would dream of me
Surrounded by curses again
Cages bind me
As history repeats before me

We used to come here
It was a wonderful place
The times have changed
Unexpected
The pollution of the industry

A soul died here
It is in the air
We stand before Dead Man's Creek
But it's felt everywhere

Today I walk another's path
For I cannot revisit
The creek still speaks to me
With too many memories
I hope they dredge the bottom
To dissipate the emptiness
To watch the sorrow drain
For so long I've had this conviction

There will be a someday
When the creek is in preservation
Those with power restore tradition
Returning it to it's natural condition

WE ARE NOT IN LOVE

A claim of truth
A quitclaim of desire
I'm the star fool
In an audience of fools

Climbing the hill countless times
Taking the thrill ride everyday
Engaged in limitless conversation
Setting the bar higher for descendants

A new addendum to passion's policy
All along feeling guided from above
Never a better feeling than this one
We are not in love

You dove head first into a brick layered foundation
Hoping it would turn out pliable
You crashed and nestled in
Fighting the desire to realize your mistake

I thought you were happy
Now I suffer your lapse of reason
I have to let you go
And I don't know how

For the first time I face my enemies
For the second time I face my demons
I cannot wish this away when difficult and tedious
I cannot be like you

Whilst swimming in empty seas
We wondered what was below the surface
We both knew we were thinking the same thing
By looking at the other

In a class all by ourselves
What outsiders say they can only dream of
A force that has become impenetrable
We are not in love

WORLDS APART

Nomadic, nebular, sporadic
In and out of reality
Lateral and parallel of feelings
I never cross them in travel

Where you are
How you got there
What you are doing now?
I shudder and wake from my stupor
I'm back to things I can control

Bird in a rainbow
Finds his gold
All I receive is the rain
Limitless, protective and overbearing
Are the defenders of my heart
Misconstrued, despondent, reflective
As we now stand worlds apart

THROWING DICE

He looks out to the city on the horizon
His dreams have died there on many occasions
The cycle repeats
As he's moves thirty miles away
Still he feels the rush
The shiver of non-forgiveness
Scaling the city walls of the future
Finding there is no top floor

Amongst a multitude of cohorts
Surrounded by those with interest invested
The dream pursued so long now obtained
Somehow it doesn't feel right

Uncertain where the bird should land
Or when the wind will stop blowing
Like a kite let go in the sky
Shifting with every current

Making the best of the situation
Attempts to convince himself
Never to think in the years of his life
That a calculated risk is like throwing dice

OUT OF SEASON

I am homebound with humanity,
As you shop for future ideas and emotions,
Changing your views and life's notions,
At one time laid to rest
Dialogue that involves me today,
Tossed as the committee constructs their decision,
All choices planned with precision,
Though you don't see it that way,

The captain is briefed about the weather,
After deliberation, he changes their direction,
The crew displays defection,
Because they didn't decide together,

A bird in the trees stops singing,
For days he was content,
Leaving with the flock was his intent,
He ignored the flight patterns and they are now gone;

I held on to hope and reason
I took the stake of our future for granted
I never thought we would fall out of season
I never thought you'd become disenchanted

MY PROBLEM TOO

Rain on the windshield, rain on my heart
The winter misses the sun
I have right here and now
There is nothing left behind

Reality didn't cause the wound
It's that I didn't see it
Knowing there's more to cloudy skies
As I know there is more to your story

You've left me with nothing else
At least I deserve the truth
That's all I've ever asked
That's all I've ever wanted

You'd think I was eternally angry
You'd think I was violent
You'd think I was evil
By the way this went down

Emotions walked on
Thrown away as if useless
When did I anger the world?
Where did I go wrong?

You say it's a problem with you
This is your decision
I know that makes it easier for you
But it's still my problem too

HYPNOTIZED

So here we are on the last day
Feeling like the first day
Like we have never met
Right now I could wish that

I can't help but look back
At least I had a chance
Contemplation and rationalization
No send off or celebration

I can't hold on to ancient times
I have to let go with both hands
I hope to see that same look someone else's eyes
Until that day I'm hypnotized

LET YOU IN

Outside in
My warm bed is the cold ground
The snow my blanket
I hibernate with everyone around

The cold is out
The cold within
Ruins are everywhere
Nowhere to take shelter

Look what I have become
Disgraced by the slightest arrhythmia
Chocked full of humiliation and regret
Why would you want me to let you in?

History made but not witnessed
Impressionable actions never impressed
Who did I run into for our term of years?
Where have you gone to so suddenly?

In spite of my imagery
I can see through your armor
I can see the truth underneath
We do not speak reality

Why should I let you in?
When you forced me out?
Here we both stand
Not getting what we want

Under attack from foreign troops
You let them in under my radar
You preach of strengthening defenses
And exiling yourself for 10 years

I saw it all over your face
I read it between your lines
This was all strategized
In your written book of predictions

When your history repeats
And you've changed your mind one too many times
When you are then left out in the cold
Don't expect me to let you in

SOMETHING YOU SHOULD HAVE SAID

I found a quiet place on Idaho ave
I started digging in the dirt
As I was looking for bones
I noticed the older I get, the better I was

My hands broke the earth
Somewhere a sinkhole lies below us
Excavations find a river of blood
Leading to where the devil resides

The leaves are falling off the majestic tree
The undefeated suffers its first loss
Now a side note in time
Of a Nostradamic prognostication

A deluge of lies illustrates my reflection
While the river of truth is dammed up ahead
A spontaneous readiness to merge
By the mere echo of something you should have said

LIGHT MY WAY

Light my way tonight
Along the avenue of planets aligned
Yesterday memories are ancient
Fallen in today's ruins
Over the ground like sand
Reflected in moonlight
Light my way tonight

The wind is punishing
Am I the lost one now?
Or have I just been found?
Forces beyond control
Tackle me to the ground
I'm left with battle scars
Complimented with a call for help
But no one is in sight
Light my way tonight

The direction I now take
Shouldn't have to be an option
A peaking visionary
Couldn't have foreshadowed this wreckage
I'm in the holy land of opportunity
With the truth of my life just out of my sight
Light my way tonight

Despite the sunset and its limitations
There is a new reason to hope
I try to pull back my sanity
Hanging at the end of my rope
Even with the bitter cold
Your existence will be put right
Light my way tonight

ONE MORE DAY

Closed in, knocked down, but fighting
Nature abhors a vacuum
Intelligence has been killed
Ignorance remains

I am simple, I have convictions
Nothing to release me from habit
Like clockwork I'm the missionary
I deliver good news despite the truth

Not dead but not alive
A motionless way of life
Lies were witnessed before
It's all come back to you

I'm more than disregarded
In a state of ramification
Distractions rampant inside
Unable to finish what was started

Simply following suit
Without the jack-of-all-trades
I've become much too forgiving
A shadow with too many shades

Starting on the little rock
Pacing on the stepping stones
Parts of me so far ahead
Other parts desolately alone

No way to understand
Somehow beyond the horizon
Still missing after years of searching
The time has come to cease fighting

One more day to hope
To give into confidence
Tomorrow it all becomes clear
One more day to believe it can be done

SCAPEGOAT AND THE INSTIGATOR

You keep throwing sunlight at me
While your garden is shaded by trees
I found my way to your fortress walls
Your defenses now aimed at me

My view is distorted
As far back as I can recall
I am retained for trespassing
Caught scaling your wall

Charged with running too fast
While I've been still for years
Finding fossils in your imperial dirt
Where there was a rumored past

Waiting for your declaration
From the attempt at truths appeal
Preaching of lies precedes you
Stamped with an official seal

Feedback on your message
Sounds of an imposter
As if a phantom possessed your body
You've become the scapegoat and the instigator

6 DAYS

You'd think it a welcomed truce
Possibly a cease-fire
No contact from either side
No indication it will expire

You accused me of standing ground
In combat born of your aggression
An obvious detail overlooked
Suitable for your sustained indiscretion

The first day was most difficult
The second builds on the first
The third becomes a competition
To see if I can make matters worse
The fourth rids me of my culpability
The fifth hints of a new approach
On the sixth day I don't care anymore
Deeming all others worthwhile

YOU JUST DON'T FEEL THAT WAY ANYMORE

In relevant circumstances
It may have been irrelevant
In some communities
It might have been a crime
You cannot force the sun to come out
You cannot stop the rain

I cannot change waiting at the corner
I cannot change that it was all in vain
I cannot help thinking
History has taught me nothing again

The mediaplex of feelings
Surround the midpoint
Thinking of visions passed
Everything lucid in retrospection

Drawing an understanding
With the symbol of my mind
Years in the making
Complimented with a waste of time
I could do what I should have done long before
But you just don't feel that way anymore

A MARCHING ARMY

A marching army
With waves rolling westward
Sending a message
From the other side of the world
Eternally peaceful and deadly
Inviting and threatening
In its wake time expands
As it makes acquaintances with the sand

Silence, then thunder
Greeting with each wave
Intensifying piece of mind
Inducement to stay
Here everything is celebrated
There is a coveted tranquility
Here there are no voices
Just a place for silence to fall

The beaches are empty
The streets are vacant
In a disloyalty
With a forgiving peace

Here there is no commemoration
Here there are no fears
Just the wind, sky and ocean
And millions of years

WAITING

Acceptance of a stipulation
In the mezzanine of my soul
The dirge rings out until its end
An issue reaches conciliation

The trite abuse of my communal heart
Law of hedonism is passed
My hegira will be the undertaking
I am still here waiting

This is not to sound morose
But this way of life I am ready to dispose
I'm not a plowboy for the labor
Nor a poster boy for cutting irony

The summons scheduled for a specific time
The day slowly arrived
It now feels improbable
As the last of shadows cast on the sundial

If you want to make the myth a legend
I'm repositioned if not timorous
The day preceding ever so prodigal
As I linger in readiness and expectation

The arc of understanding diminished
With each breath anticipating
I expected annihilation by now
But I am still here waiting

LEAVING FLORIDA

It has become an attribute
We've grown mutually, indissoluble
A fragment stays behind
Heartrending to get here and to leave

A resident alien
I made this town my own
So far from fluency and familiarity
I've organized my place of abode

Irreprehensible, indispensable
Irresponsible, unconscionable
Much maligned but impressionable
Leaving Florida

Now I make my way home
As my memories are shipped to Mexico
Lost without them at my expense
Unable to use them nevertheless

Discourse, dissolution
Irreconcilable, incontestable
Misled but not misguided
Leaving Florida

You went missing
I remained where I am
Yet you stayed
I'm thousands of miles away

An outsider in my own skin
Waiting out the storm you've ushered in
Previously outsmarting these conditions
But I was too credulous this time

Suspenseful anticipation
Mourning and celebration
Caged emancipation
Leaving Florida

Dust and debris settled
Here I'm no longer enviable
Everywhere the same sentiment
My tour of duty fulfilled

Ironic, histrionic
Anything but platonic
Regrettable but remarkable
Leaving Florida

In the final stretch of the imagination
The sun's curtain call to the west
What's behind stays behind
Everything else fades out

Pretentious, conscientious, defenseless
Graceless, pointless, ludibrious
Motionless and emotionless
Leaving Florida

RIGHT TIME OF DAY, RIGHT TIME OF YEAR

20 miles west of the young town
Wheels hug the turnpike ground
Eyes are heavy, mind still shut down
Light infringement all around

I get a chance in fall
To answer the road's call
No intention outright
No looking back within sight

I will be home in a day
A place I've come to forget
My whole process revamped
To a town I haven't set foot in yet

But what is behind and ahead
Makes no matter right here
As the turning leaves reflect in the dawn
It's the right time of day, right time of year

My mind can't fake the effort anymore
I see what I have to do
The year's end much longer than before
Compounds with what I've been through

A gripping story of survival
Without a cliffhanger ending
An excuse laden trial
With a life that was just pretending

In an instant my mind snaps back
As the colors of this painting soak in my mind
For now I have nothing to fear
Right time of day, right time of year

BEGIN

Star in the night
Gone before day
I should have toyed with the prospect
That you were meant to go your own way

Call me fanatical
I look for what isn't there
Call me insensible
I was destined to no longer care

Stay the night or pack your bags
Either way we're a step closer
The thunder from the terminal
Reminds us it is time

This was never the solution
But the excuses have intensified
We face a verse in our history
With no lines scripted

I put you under a microscope
Because you gave me a reason
We signed off on the same treaty
Then you committed treason

I like to believe I'm am above suspicion
But guilt is now my best friend
You're not the only one
To ride a train of thought to it's end

I could set this free
After I towed you through my recovery
Now your choices are your own
I'm left to my new discovery

This will come to pass
What will become of you?
I hope your rose colored glasses
Have lenses you can see through

In the starless night
Trails remain of our jet engine
I see the moon and sun
A new era is about to begin

NOTHING UNDERNEATH

Black smoke rising
From this distance
I can only see the sun's cylinder shape
But darkness has fallen at noon

Straddled under encumbrances
Blacklisting my wisdom
Faith is on my side
But it has fallen behind

Evacuation of the building
All my belongings destroyed
There is nowhere left I know
As I stare you down

You pledged this fealty
I was taken by the theft of reason
I was awed by the shooting stars
I was fooled by the beauty of the season

There are now excuses to be made
And a mess to clean up
The fire burned the edges of reality
I'm left with not enough

There is a subtle fury abroad
The docile has gone on the attack
Where was the rainbow I chased before?
This prism only shows black

The portion that is certainty
Outweighed by belief
I've peeled away all the layers
There is nothing underneath

LACK OF EVERYTHING

It has taken shape
The day before and after
It has caused me
To come out of this
Shaken and stirred
A misshapen reflection
A doubtful coronation
A whimsical reaction

A gaping hole
Caused by our lack of everything
The devil holds his own
There's no need to help him along

It has taken me
It has thrown me out
Two days past relevance
Days before I knew

The sun goes down
Leaving night shadows
Returning again
Threatening to remain

Guilt is an alleyway
Guilt is a ravine
I have fallen into
Never to be seen

This deity shaped hole
Cause by our lack of patience
When you see the devil
Don't give him motivation

These days I tend to recognize
I tend to fight
The world is much bigger
Than an individual plight

But the world also knows
More than it leads on to
An ultimate goal
That has already taken action

I try to fill it up
With something I believe in
Something that brings forgiveness
Before it's too late

LOST IN THE WORLD

I had a dream you went across country
That you thought about more than yourself
Somehow you wind up in on the East Coast
Hoping to figure it out

With egos higher than mountains
You skied off the steepest slope
Landing on everyone who believed in you
Standing at the bottom alone

Being impressed isn't enough
If there are no amends
You cannot ravage everything
When there are limits on how you treat friends

You're still lost in the world
Yet to receive enlightenment
Your river as shallow as before
Up to your neck at the shore

Now I stand on the mountain
I see you wandering in the distance
Too proud to ask for directions
Too stubborn to ask for forgiveness

I will reach out my hand
I hope to see you again someday
If you climb from your river to the sand
Then the past might drift away

BLIND SPOTS

Blind spots in my mental picture
I cannot see beyond
Clouding authenticity
Contorting certainty
The blue is always black
It is what I anticipate
Now it is all I see
Inaccuracy with precision

You hover over this abandoned space
You gravitate towards the blind spots
I'm getting used to your passage
I'm diminished, I understand
Mostly I cannot see you
But I can feel you taking pieces of me
I sense you're leaving the emptiness
I feel nothing in your place

Blind spots before me
Dark spots on the horizon
Corrupting your image
And everything to come
You worship indifference
Clearing your mind and memory
Your dreams are initiated
The negative phased out
I pick up the pieces
I make allowances for what you have done
These blind spots have taken over
With accuracy and precision
I no longer see anything or anyone

I KNOW HIM, SHE KNOWS YOU

I look at you for the first time
I know you know
You read my face as I read yours
We try to pretend we just met
You've heard past stories
You are in the loop
You are informed
I pretend I don't know you know

I know him and she knows you
Two separate lives before you
Bound together by the oddest of situations
A well-known secret to everyone
I suspect I am a topic
I hope you say I am doing well
I wonder if you mention me
I wonder if she asks

More than likely you remain silent
The one that knows more than anyone
You think it's not your business
But you are in the thick of it
My heart hurts
I make sure you'll never know
Or have anything to report

We four are in an inimitable position
No one else understands
It is still a mystery
We've stopped asking questions
Everyone plays the fool
Hoping it will go away
Hoping we will all forget
That I know him and she knows you

SECOND HAND MAN

You thought it would be different this time
Instead you've proven that nothing is sacred
No veneration for something she couldn't honor
You thought she wouldn't change her mind again

Second hand job, second hand band
Second hand woman, second hand man
I need a third hand to count the reasons I'm embarrassed for you
Thank you for the ammunition that she chose to shoot

I hope you're happy when she leaves again
I hope it was worth being the whipping boy again
In the blink of an eye your hands will be empty again
She won't be satisfied with the money you spend

Thank you for playing the part of the vulture
In a play that criticized everything I believed in
You obviously have no reserves about being the fool again
Thank you for confirming my suspicion

NOTHING NEW

The sickness takes hold
The storm comes in
A plague ending all plagues
A new level of sin

I have been failed
We failed each other
The world might end tomorrow
But I'm still here now

Destroy my conscience and confidence
Disregard my legacy
Deny all of my truths
Suffocate my hopes and dreams
Take my last breath
Unravel me at the seams
Drag my body through the dungeons
Throw my bones to the fire
Erase me from existence
Deny everything proven true
Obliterate my kingdom despite my resistance
It will be nothing new

On the verge of tomorrow
I'll know everything about you
You will be a liar
It will be nothing new

SEASON OF ARMISTICE

Inanimate emotions
Stranded on a neighborless shore
Unconstitutional obligation
Ultimately leading to war

A violation now elapsed
For psychological treason
Soliciting a pardon agreement
In abandoned prisons

Previous prognostication
Belligerence begets belligerence
Ardor for a soldier archetype
Despite the season of armistice

Approbation of inhumanity
Assuaged by camaraderie
Once a shimmer of shortcomings
Becoming an uncouth glare

A vendetta now served
No advantage earned
Searching for character
In a characterless assemblage

Today I am left with fragments
As I begin to devaluate
Waiting for the cliché
With one half diabolic

Remaining solvent and resonant
In spite of the divination
Foreordained for greatness
Claims this enduring sentience

HAPPEN

For just one moment
I felt my spirit weaken
Certain it would ensue

I endeavored to reclaim my sanity
Remove my infirmity
Knowing it would come to pass
You cannot stay in this place
This place I call my mind
You cannot remain here with me
When you've crossed to the other side

For just one moment
My dreams were a map leading you to me
I knew it wouldn't happen

When I saw the sunrise
I thought the day could bring new light
I realized it couldn't come about today
It won't revolutionize
Until I ask what I'm afraid to ask
Only then will I be free

Until I can look you in the eye
I will stay here in hell's prison
With the fire at my feet

So here we are now
Face to face for the millionth time
Will I rise to the occasion?
Or let another opportunity die?
As I'm walking away again
I see your taillights fade
I wait for the next time
I make believe I'm heroic

It won't vary
Until I put my sanity at stake
Only then can I face explanation
Next time I will tell you
That I've known all along
We could have tried to save each other
But we knew it wouldn't happen

FINAL CHAPTER

Still feels like home
I'd be admonished for these thoughts
When the forces of nature are contended
We will always go down

Change of locks, change of heart
Eternal optimism missing from the start
All the plot lines and feelings fall from the rafters
We've reached our last chapter

A return to well being and shelter
You perceive me as the aggressor
Though you have all the artillery
I'm put on trial because I suffer

A response of indifference
Behind the scenes action is contradiction
Not disparate to anything else you are
As I can only stand and bear witness

I didn't mean to throw daggers
You're the one who drew blood
You danced for rain
I'm the one drowning in the flood

Today I look in retrospection
I've read all the pages in between
I won't know if you were genuine
Or just another actor
We've closed the final chapter.

IN HELL

Shadows creeping and crawling
Out of the firelight
I find my way through the rain
Turning from your shelter
Don't spin this on me
I don't break the earth when I walk
I've been staying on course
With eyes straight ahead

You exposed me to your disease
You ignited the flame that caused the fire
I was in your cheering section for a long time
But my voice began to tire

You continue to verbalize
I can no longer hear
Nighttime falls again
Nothing is clear
Confabulation in blue haze
Creates your perfunctory fear
Your long rehearsed harangue
Comes from the encomium I hear

You say you'll be in hell
If I should not forgive you
So I bid you farewell
Have fun in hell

WORLD OF EXCUSES

Preaching the world as he knows it
Filing for the right to pray
Speaking of stars when his expertise is the moon
Warning of midnight at noon

Clocking the speed of butterflies
She pretends she is fulfilled
The velocity of regret
Captures her in her net

I'm just a non-believer
Learning in intervals
Making evolutionary leaps
With shackles around my wrists

We are not on the same frequency
We probably never were
Caught in the essence of fiction
Hoping for a momentary stir

The nighttime scavengers of the mind
Feast at my last bit of sanity
Tearing down everything with meaning
Leaving me with vanity

You remain standing tall
As long as you have your muses
Equipped with a mansion of reason
And a world of excuses

IMAGE OF YOU

Something intangible
Unfound in majority
Setting you apart
I see you in my head
I see your past actions
I relive all you've done
I'm searching for this image of you

It could be far removed
You're supposed to be the one I remember
At your most flawless
I see what serves delusion

Ten years and a happenstance return
Coincidence besieges us both
Again we are face to face
I'm thrown into the past
I apprise the situation
I can feel the rebel underneath
Blanketed by your family values

Unable to live up to my memory
I did not see it coming
I attempt to retain my reaction
The problem has now broken down
As a misguided emotion
That evolves into reminiscence
I was in love with my image of you

MY HEART LEFT TOWN

Sleep in the shallow sky
It falls into your eyes
You stole the clouds
And left your lies

I'm not to be grazed on
I'd never give my child a fake gun
I've been let down too
You're not the only one

Over your horizon
Of this long year city town
I fall from perils
Taken by surprise

I used to be the builders
I used to see the stars
Now I see pavement
Where there were once green pastures

Now I am the whistleblower
I am the martyr
I am the bullet
Missing from your gun

A paycheck and a handshake
Never solid servitude
Interminable generosity
Is only considered rude

Now you're condescending
The offering is your last word
Leave them in a letter
It's nothing I haven't heard

The stakes are much higher
Than deeper pockets
I proceed to bow out
While I can still breathe in

Who will you have to fool?
Whose head will you have to hold down?
I've learned to breath underwater
But I won't be around

You'll look into dungeons
And into the lost and found
You'll never find what you're seeking
My heart left town

THE WAY I ALWAYS DO

I couldn't see through the smoke
But I heard a familiar tune
She walked back to her seat
I didn't get up like I used to

How could it be her seat?
It doesn't have her name
Still she yells at the trespass
As if she bought it

She turned her head and smiled
Looking right at me
I turned away
Pretending not to see

Frustration set in
I compete with myself again
I'm afraid to take a stand
I'd rather be a mystery

I walked to the jukebox
She recognized the tune
As if she knew what I would do
This time we exchanged smiles

She danced alone
She mouthed "good choice" but I already knew
She was the most beautiful thing I have seen
But I didn't go home with her the way I always do

She let loose and confronted
I took the blame foresighted
She stood her ground with her mind ignited
I turned away

Just keep your distance these days
I didn't do, I only feared
It was your self-fulfilling prophecy
My conscience has been cleared

Where is the anger and sadness?
What is this indifference I've fallen into?
The worse you could've done was the worse you did
I just don't care the way I used do.

NEW DAY

Reminiscent of a detonation
I begin to feel it again
Those afraid to exist
Always suffer the fallout

I start to turn my hand
Bringing it into my vision
An easing of tension
The numbness dissipates

The awakening continues
Amongst the curious onlookers
Focusing on every move
As if they've never witnessed revivification

These eyes have stories to recount
Now a voice to commune
Willingness to extend further
As I'm welcomed back to life

One day I might elucidate
One day when there is wisdom gained
The future sun is rising
I cannot miss its coronation

The past has lessons to teach
With pitfalls and traps to evade
Though I am appreciative for learning the hard way
I'm thankful for the new day

WITHIN REACH

Reality amasses my outcome
Pleading I do not fade
Blinded by the time before this one
Contented by something I hoped to say

If you ever know my true name
Through all of the obscurity unsaid
I will know my direction
With a place to rest my head

More than knowing
A language I cannot speak
Throughout the night the moon is glowing
The garden of pleading is left to the weak

The green in my vision
Matches the palest gray
You sketch the brightest colors on your canvass
Perceived in a different way

Here stand the bricklayers of eternity
The mortar is faith in each other
Millions of buildings are constructed
Standing tall in the worst of weather

Hope is eternally animate
Akin to the blood in my veins
Always there is more to be done
I am indebted with each day

I feel contact of humanity
Yet to be condemned or sentenced
The new up is down
From pedestals we've petitioned

I live out the feeble
To find my durable
Offerings of time lead my way
To a pioneering visualization

The curtain yet to be drawn
Deficient in volunteers
Still a new beginning within reach
Looking to be better than the old

FAITH IN THE TRUTH

Something to keep you going
To shield the harsher facets
Something providing illumination
Easing the darkest judgment

A way to calm the weather
To relax the tensions
A beacon in the night
From a wishable star

The towers of aimlessness
Knocked over by gusts of conviction
Everyone has faith in something
My faith is in the truth

So much on one side of the scale
Upheaval, discontent, confusion
Hatred, violence, disillusion
Fury and dishonesty in profusion
All overshadowed by faith

Lies run unfathomable
Like magma of being
Lies beget lies
Towering into firmament

We can come full circle
Hope can run just as deep
There is wisdom, there is youth
Everyone believes in something
My faith is in the truth
My faith is in you

CELEBRATION AND TRAGEDY

Celebration and tragedy
Intertwined like roots of existence
Delivered in mysterious balance
A celebratory fool is always anxious
He knows what is next
The pleasure now is part of the pain later
The two indivisible
Departure of belief only leads to ignorance

This was hardly growing old together
I will miss you interminably
If you could observe me now
You'd come down from where you are
I watch as angels receive you

I struggle to be appreciative
I endeavor to recognize your sacrifice
Opting to spend your time on earth in my company
I strive to be in celebration
Instead of tragedy

Could you save me the closing dance?
I give my existence more than a passing glance
I was going to set aside what I have to say
But tomorrow may be today

Celebration and tragedy
Intertwined like roots of eternity
No more living in yesterday
While watching the now slip away

If you should you be fixed in tragedy
Expect that it breeds acceptance in duration
Be assured in the balance of inevitability
Next in line will be celebration

PHOTOGRAPHS

We are here now
Waiting for a moment
Time expands to days
You with your eyes gazing
As if you've invented sight
Me at the edge of my patience

Counting down until right now
Living harder in the time here
Recollection of each day
For all the time that it is
Knowing we have to return
To the normalcy of life

Aspiring for a break in time
Hoping to slow it down
Taking mental photographs
When the day comes to leave
Returning to the dark room of our minds
To develop the memories

The way the water rippled to our feet
While sitting at the edge of the world
The way the air felt untouched
As life begins rehabilitation

The final days encircle us
Though not to force a scowl
The journey to the proverbial back home
Begins the machinations of another itinerary
Until then we have the photographs
Developed in our minds

ONE ROAD

You are split ends and decisions
I am for sale with a contract bid
You are a one-way street in the wrong direction
A high authority accused of defection

You're too smart to know anything
Too confused to be indecisive
You veer off and can't get back
Your exit sign is revealed after it's already passed

You are the intersection
But not the continuance
You're the short-lived thrill
But not the persistence

You are all over the place
Changing names in every town
My yellow lines might be faded and old
At least I have always been one road

I've invested money into this turnpike tollbooth
I was in for the long haul
I thought this was the only passage
But I find an alternate route after all

Now you're a designated escape route
A chosen role reversed
Passers by know your history
They believe your viaduct as cursed

You are the traffic jam
You are the nuance
You are the easy way out
You are the path of least resistance

You are the down and out
But not the reprieve
I am supposed to accept
Without an option to grieve

In the end we both travel alone
Your rules and routes are constantly changing
Your asphalt requires a new code
I can sleep at night knowing I've always been one road

NOT A DRY EYE IN THE HOUSE

Not a dry eye in the house
As they take one last bow
Movement towards the exit
The night has reached its ending

An astonishing turn of events
A chilling ending for the story line
A plot twist like no other
Leaving them speechless

Magnificently misunderstood
Creatively misinterpreted
Consequently inevitable
Beautifully lost in repugnance

Not a dry eye in the house
As they reminisce
Hoping for a continuation
Where could it possibly go from here?

SMOKESCREEN

It's time I start lying about my age
It's time to start slipping under radar
I'm glad you've fallen for my cover story
But there is definitely more to tell you

Far away and long ago
You wouldn't have ever known me
Time stabbed me in the back recently
I'm still recovering from the wound

Forced out of my hole
Where I usually run and hide
I need a little nudge now and then
My agent of change paved the way

Now I'm here in front of you
Life has become much more valuable
It's the moments in between
Making it worthwhile

That is why I flashed my keys
That is why I flashed credentials
Not to simply impress
But to hope you'd see through the smokescreen

There is more to me than I can show today
As I know there is more to you
I slide the piece of paper across the table
Hoping you will call

Maybe you can change my opinion
I'm hopeful at this outcome
I can still see the look in your eyes
As I remain in anticipation

I'm willing to try it all again
Even though I have had a bad run at it
What I thought was true before
Was really just a smokescreen

DUAL IDENTITY

I am misconception
I am like a hooker
I run the corporate gamut by day
Triumphant home wrecker by night

You will not find the right words
Your other significant impugns you for me
Let it go because there's no excuse
I'm the one you want to be

I am a pop star
Likened to those I give credit too
The night falls and I'm in metamorphosis
There are two of me that you don't know

I am identical
To the 9 to 5 commodity
I am the Hyde to that Jeckyl
To my pearl of great price

You walk in the door
You hear a voice resonating off the walls
As you make your way around the corner
Your acceptance befalls

You now stand before my secret
A surreal test of the moment
It's as if it cannot register
The penny for your thoughts

It's time to push the boundaries
There's more to me than you allow
I need more than 9 to 5
I have sought and I did find

The night will end and the set will close
You will see me Monday
A passing glance between us will speak volumes
Even if no one else knows

I am a superhero
The two identities won't overlap
Night and weekends I expand
On weekday's I snap back

Time for you to walk away
Stop wishing you acknowledged me before
I'm who I've been everyday
You're the one who should have been more

THE DIFFERENCE

I was at one time deceived
Combating devils whilst angels fell
Standing on the brink of distinction
Torn between heaven and hell

I staved off the wars of elders
Avoiding pit falls of hypocrisy
All of the hindrances that hinge on failure
Were unable to puncture my drogue of intention

Still there was a parallel
With one misstep I might have veered off
Wherewithal of altering my entire motif
Obliteration from a simple belief

If not for your magnetic pull
I would not have discovered my north
Or witnessed the victory of reality
While arriving to this final lucidity

Amidst the collapse of disillusionment
You have become my minds eye
You are my sixth sense
You are the difference

THE END OF AND ERA

Last time keeping this space
That I declare my own
Last time walking through this archway
This is no longer my home

Last time criticizing and complimenting
As only I can do
The long years felt diminutive in conclusion
As soon as our time here was through

Last time for atonement
Because of something I could never do
We've tipped the scales on both sides
Ignoring the weight of what is true

Last time for acquiescence and being fooled
Despite the numerous believable pleas
Last time thinking I'm irreprehensible
For the destruction of the seas

Last time looking back to you
For what I now can find in myself
Your mind is now in bankruptcy
As I'm searching for mental wealth

Last time thinking I am superior
To the person in front of me
Last time visiting the grave
Of all that I used to believe

SERIES OF HYPOTHETICALS

The day begins to darken
As the train begins its boarding
A new remedy for the disaster
Has already emerged

No time to properly say goodbye
Something I wasn't sure how to do
A blind fool fumbling around in the dark
As I watch you move out of my view

My heart increases pace
With the speed on the track
With the thought of you on my mind
And the thought of coming back

There is something more to this
There is something about you
It is something more than I've ever expected
It is something more than I ever knew

Please forgive my series of hypotheticals
I'm always ahead of myself
I don't mean to push the envelope
I don't meant to push for answers

What the forces unite
Distance cannot divide
A feeling of confidence
That this sentiment won't break stride

The machine slows itself
I step off as it trails away
Of one thing I am certain
A new life begins here today.

THE END